Dis.Masterpieces.

damian willcox

"DISASTERPIECES"
© 2017 damian willcox
published by dorkboy comics in canada
www.dorkboycomics.com

short excerpts may be reproduced for review purposes.
contact: damian@dorkboycomics.com

Introduction.

When I first started making comics, everything fit nicely under a single comic title, 'dorkboy'... but as time went on I seem to have invented more and more comic characters, spanned more mediums, interests and formats. This has helped maintain my enthusiasm and exploration in cartoons (while simultaneously either entertaining or confusing fans, I'm sure), but has made naming my books a little more interesting also.

Gone are the days when the next book would simply be dorkboy #7.1 or 8.1 or 9.1. At this point, my books are more of a yearbook collecting the most recent adventures of characters on my drawing pages, as well as myself. Some years have clear themes such as "Zillas Ruining Classic Art" (which I drew in its entirety laying on the living room floor

while dealing with some back problems that went on far too long). But this year, the title was less obvious for me. It would eventually come to me I told myself, and I was almost entirely certain it would contain a pun because me and puns go WAAAY back.

Somewhere along the line, the presence of the destructive Zillas that permeate my cartoons, my sick addiction to puns, and the irony in the fact that I would never ever dare term anything I have done as a 'Masterpiece' brought me to 'Disasterpieces'...and it might be the best description of my work yet.

I hope these 'Disasterpieces' bring you a smile, chuckle, or even a fleeting groan at one of my terrible, terrible puns. Most of all, I really hope you enjoy the pages ahead.

Thanks,

♥damian

Inktober.

For Inktober this year (a month of daily ink drawings), I decided to put in a more concerted effort. Instead of 'quick' sketches to meet the daily quota, I dedicated time and effort to finish with a month of works I could be relatively happy with...or at least not overly unhappy with.

Anyone that follows me online will likely recognize that once I start a drawing theme I tend to run with it... perhaps way, way too far. Inktober this year was no exception. I primarily took aim at the early James Bond era secret agents from yesteryear - classy, dangerous, beautiful & timeless. Aaaaand then, somehow or other I ended up adding Zillas to the mix. I have a problem. As I worked through Inktober, to get a sense of if I liked an idea or not I would make a quick Sharpie sketch (below), and if so I would proceed on to a better version. You can also see some 'in progress' Inktobers on this page to prove that I actually do sort of pencil sometimes before inking (but I avoid it as much as possible).

← my brush pen

Inktober was created by Jake Parker, and involves creating daily drawings with ink during the month of October. Find out more at **mrjakeparker.com**

Secret Agent 001

(I started off my first Inktober with a bit of a classic spy theme that continued throughout. All of them use brushpen with black ink and some white highlights)

Secret Agent 002

(I aimed for a 60s/70s feel to a lot of these - hence the psychedelic background on this one. Or maybe that's just a nod to Austin Powers)

Secret Agent 003

(Classic Bond martini in this one, and I did my best to try hiding the agent number in the images also - note the '003' on the matchbox)

Secret Agent 004

"It was said that by the time you heard Secret Agent 004, it was far, far too late..." *(I had a LOT of fun incorporating the 'Inktober' title in each one)*

Secret Agent 005

"Secret Agent 005 would ALWAYS live to fight another day"

(I began to shade with the one Copic marker I owned around this time)

Secret Agent 006

"Secret Agent 006 wondered if this feeling was love...but then decided it was unrequited love, as she hadn't brought the antidote."

Secret Agent 007

"Secret Agent 007 was infamous for his poker face...his companions didn't always share this talent however..."

Secret Agent 008

"Secret Agent 008 was developing serious allergies to henchmen."

(you can faintly see the '008' in the dress, and Inktober on the ledge)

Secret Agent 009

"Sure, Secret Agent 009 had to make the document drop, but there was no reason to not enjoy a scoot on an otherwise beautiful day."

Secret Agent 010

"Secret Agent 010 could remember Q laughing at him (or maybe he called him an alcoholic) when he requested a custom pen that could display a martini hologram."

Secret Agent 011

"Secret Agent 011 loved it when her lucky numbers came up in a combination." *(my marker collection grew as the month went on...)*

Secret Agent 012

"Secret Agent 012 couldn't shake the feeling that his state of the art
miniature jet pack was actually more noticeable than Q had let on..."

Secret Agent 013

"Secret Agent 013 had many skills: Elizabethan Actor, Improvisational Dancer, Scintillating Conversationalist, Secret Agent....in that order."

Secret Agent 014

"Secret Agent 014 brought her utensils everywhere and absolutely
LOVED seafood...sorry about the sharks, Dr. Nope."

Secret Agent 015

"Secret Agent 015 could never remember Q's instructions for
working the radio..."

Secret Agent 016

"Secret Agent 016 was ready for man eating sea bass and poison tipped
spear wielding henchmen, but not loan sharks...not like this."

Secret Agent 017

"Secret Agent 017 maintained his cover as a photographer right up until
the moment Blofeld said 'but I am smiling'. Rest in Peace 017."

Secret Agent 018

"Secret Agent 018 would become extremely well known for this iconic pose, but he would always remember it as the day Q saved him from shooting his own nose off."

Secret Agent 019

"Secret Agent 019 had broken a long standing Spy rule - never take your eyes off of the glass you added the colourless, odourless doubleohsevenium to."

Secret Agent 020

"Secret Agent 020 may not have had a golden gun, but she did have a loaded gun... which usually gave the upper hand in the game of Thunderball."

Secret Agent 021

"Secret Agent 021 felt a bit sad as he cranked Dr. No's lair towards self destruction as he'd sure miss wearing this custom faux tuxedo radiation suit."

Secret Agent 022

"Secret Agent 022 had a sneaking suspicion that there might be a cold blooded killer at the party…" *(Zillas entered the theme at this point somehow)*

Secret Agent 023

"Secret Agent 023 had some hesitation when he accepted the Tokyo mission due to his mysterious past, but now he was almost certain he had blown his cover..."

Secret Agent 024

"Secret Agent 024 had become known as 'The Eraser',
because he could make problems disappear..."

Secret Agent 025

"Secret Agent 025 wasn't terribly good at being a spy and didn't really know how to use a snorkel, but mostly what kept him alive was the fact that he wasn't delicious."

Secret Agent 026

"Secret Agent 026 thought finding Spectre's secret volcano lair would be difficult, but getting inside would be simple....he was incorrect on both counts."

Secret Agent 027

"Secret Agent 027 was infamous for his ability to call someone's bluff, but truth be told he actually had no idea how to play poker and only came for the giant martinis."

Secret Agent 028

"Secret Agent 028 packed only the essentials for his ski vacations in the Swiss Alps - bullet proof tuxedo snowsuit...and parachute."

Secret Agent 029

"Secret Agent 029 overshot the volcanic island/underground headquarters of Spectre, and instead chose to land on the island of lackadaisical dinosaurs."

Secret Agent 030

"Secret Agent 030 discovered that Q had failed to consider anatomical shortcomings for initiating the detonation sequence from his new wristwatch."

Secret Agent 031

"Secret Agent 031 was only ever deployed on one mission where he unceremoniously misinterpreted going to the party 'in disguise'"

Zillas.

A lot of my works are actually incredibly small! Case in point, the Zilla paintings below are actual size! (See eraser for scale in photo below left)

I thought it may be of interest to include some of my work process. To the left I have my very rough 'idea' sketch. After that, I tape down my watercolour paper to give it a nice border (and prevent warping while I paint). Far left in blue is a rough transfer that I loosely follow for inking (middle), and then I add the colours with watercolour paint.

idea sketch...

rough layout...

Inking...

"Adventure awaits"

"Zilla Knievel"

"Japan Air to Zilla Flip"

"Tokyo Rodeo"

"Dropping In"

It took a lot of paint splattering to get that mess of colour in the middle, but it was fun…

"The storm before the calm"

Much like most of my work, I had no idea how this would turn out. I wanted it to be a rainy scene, but with a lot of light and reflection. This meant having to rely on the watercolours, and not the linework to make it happen...and watercolour is notoriously not to be relied on at the best of times.

"Future Primitive"

More playing with water, reflections and everything
else difficult in watercolour, haha. 'Future Primitive' is
also the name of a very old skateboarding video.

"Zilla vs the Friendly Octopus"

This started out as an idea on a post-it note. I thought it would be funny if Zilla made an unwanted friend as he emerged from the ocean to destroy the city.

Zilla/Robot Art Process

This particualr painting was done in my watercolour sketchbook. I use green painters tape (you can find it at any hardware store) directly on the sketchbook. It keeps the paint out, but doesn't stick to the paper too much and doesn't tear the paper when I peel it off.

I do very loose/rough penciling. I don't like to pencil much at all (when I do it), because I want the inking step to have a life of its own, and not simply involve tracing pencil lines. Super light pencil for rough placement of the items in the scene, and then inking with a brush pen.

For the inking step, I usually focus on the main characters first - that way if I screw them up, I can throw out the drawing sooner haha. I don't have any set rules, but usually foreground characters, then midground, and finally distant background (at least in this example). I also don't use rulers, and eyeball the perspective which is probably terrible practice. Bad artist!

And finally, the distant background: trees, plants, sky and what have you. After this I try to be patient and wait for the ink to fully dry before erasing any pencil lines. Next is watercolour, which is a blur of me trying to paint the entire thing in one sitting as I don't like to belabour that step too much. Watercolour has a mind of its own anyway.

"Once (more) Around the Park"

There are so many stories out there about robots vs monsters, but really - couldn't they be best friends? I think so.

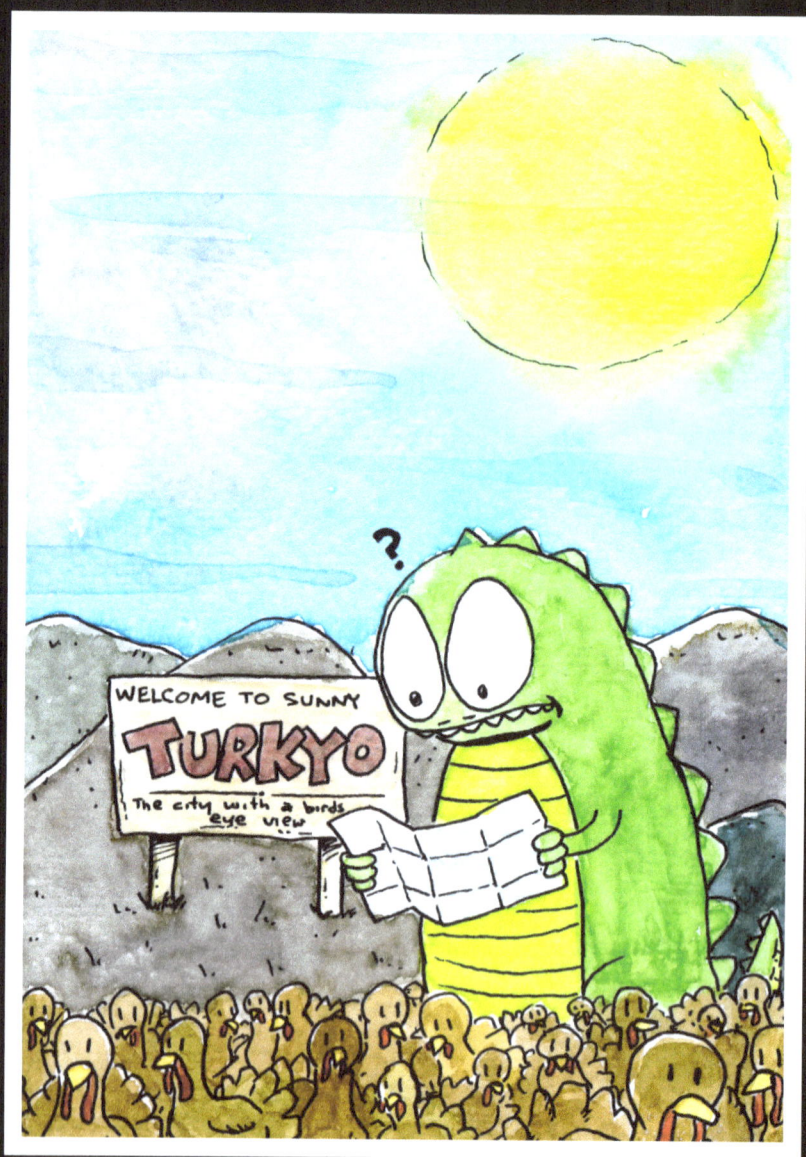

"Zilla vs GPS"

Um...I can't explain this one.

"Theory of Relativity"

I often wonder how terrified people would be if Zilla was much, MUCH smaller. (Inking stage image to the left)

"Zilla vs Time Travel"

And once again we learn that using time travel for our own self interests will only result in disappointment.

"At the height of his career"

My thought process as I made this one was, "wouldn't it be funny if Zilla was just about to destroy the city when some ridiculous obstacle that he could easily ignore stood in his way?" I thought the reveal in the second panel made the idea come together. Though, as someone pointed out to me on the internet - the incredible Gary Larson made a single panel Far Side cartoon MANY years earlier with essentially the identical premise. I don't recall ever seeing his cartoon, so this either came from deep within my subconscious memory from decades earlier....or I have a similar sense of humour which is a pretty good second option.

"Bath Time"

I painted this one while in Japan in a ¥200 ($2) sketchbook from Comiket.
It didn't really like watercolour from what I could tell.

"Zilla vs Milkra"

The city will be shaking! (Obligatory milk pun)

"Roughing it"

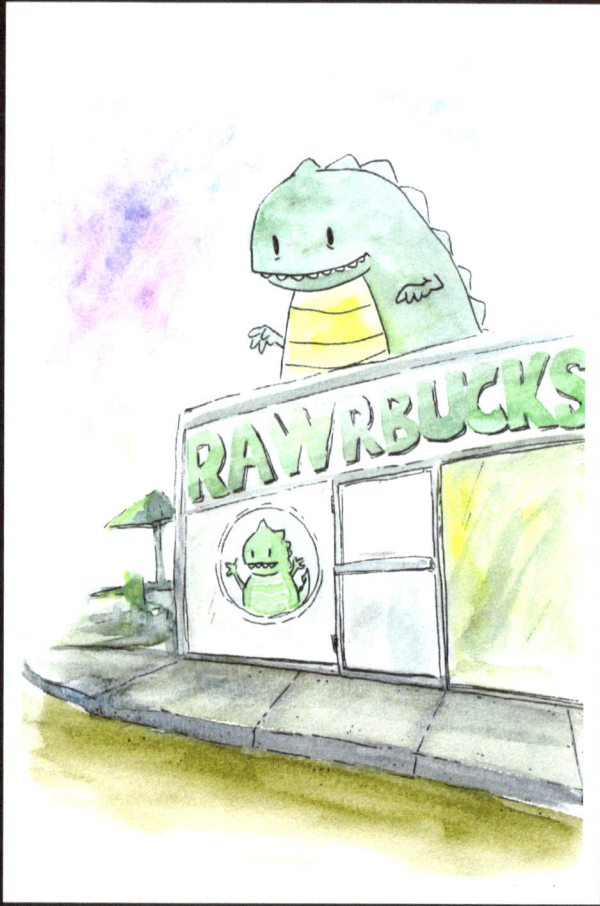

"Kaiju Latte

More of me trying to make th
sketchbook like watercolour in Japa

"Day in the City"

Refusing to give up, this
sketchbook is going to learn to
love watercolour!!

"All Weather Zilla"

My first Tryptych.
Probably my last.

Here are the little fellas taped down to my drawing table, inked, and ready to paint. Getting the positioning and size of the Zillas relatively the same took some pre-planning.

And here they are finished and untaped. My trusty eraser is shown for size - once again, these are more of my very tiny paintings. The ones above are more or less actual size.

"Hello, old friend..."

As mentioned, I think there is a strong possibility that Zillas and Robots are friends in real life.

"The Power of Love"

Alternate title "Take that, Huey Lewis".

Robots.

"You looked bigger in the movie"

That ¥200 sketchbook, now back in Canada is
starting to give up its fight against watercolour.
Victory!

"How to get a Suspension"

Robopun.

"Inkybot"

Both of these were straight to ink with a brushpen, no penciling beforehand....though I did use white ink afterwards to make the "stars".

"The funny thing was, Randall was incredibly shy about his laser cannon arm, yet couldn't stop talking with his Hand pupbot arm... "

"Lend a Hand"

"Roger tried to dismiss it as an anomaly, but when he was refused a seat the second time - in spite of now having a tie, his proximity sensors indicated that there were also no other robots in this restaurant. "

"Petal to the Metal"

And so begins a love story of robot and flower.

"Will you be waiting for me when I get out?"

The suspenseful second act!

"The Great Escape"

...and thrilling conclusion.

"Hey...who's the new kid?"

"Blind Date"

Based on a true story?

"Well there's your problem right there! You've got a broke seal!"

"Cash, Cheque or Visa?"

I went through a frustratingly long process involving multiple Visa offices and multiple rejections as I attempted to get a China Visa for a work trip. I drew this comic after it finally got accepted.

Comiket, Tokyo

On my last trip to Japan I visited Comiket! (And wore my Zilla costume!) So much to see, and a really fun show - I'm hoping one time I can sign up for a table there myself!

COMIKET

dorkboy comics presents...

by damian willcox 2017

'COMIKET' (COMIC MARKET) IS A HUGE COMIC CONVENTION HELD IN TOKYO AT THE 'BIG SIGHT' EVENT CENTER....

← COOLEST CONVENTION CENTRE

I DECIDED TO GO, BRINGING ALONG MY GODZILLA COSTUME FOR THE FULL EXPERIENCE (WHEN IN TOKYO...)

Whoa! there's a dedicated change room for costumes? fancy!

godzilla costume in back pack

ALL COSPLAY MUST PAY ¥1000 REGISTRATION FEE

USING GOOGLE TRANSLATE TO OVERCOME MY TERRIBLE JAPANESE SKILLS

I PAID THE FEE (ABOUT $10) WHICH ENDED UP BUYING ME A SMALL PIECE OF CARPET IN A CROWDED ROOM...

DON'T ASK

Wait a sec... So many bras... and make up... am I in the right change area?

AMATEUR

THEY TAKE 'COSPLAY' SUPER SERIOUSLY IN JAPAN

← EVERYONE HAD SUITCASES FILLED WITH COSTUME SUPPLIES

FIRST STOP.

HOW CAN I BE THE ONLY PERSON AT A COMIC SHOW IN TOKYO TO DRESS AS GODZILLA?

CUTE!

← GREEN ZILLA NEEDS A GREEN DRINK ...MATCHA!

STARBUCKS EMPLOYEES IN JAPAN BRING A MENU WITH PICTURES WHEN THERE'S A LINEUP AND/OR YOU'RE A FOREIGNER

ONE OF THE BEST THINGS ABOUT COMIKET IS THE HUGE DIVERSITY OF CREATORS - YOUNG AND OLD, MALE AND EVEN MORE FEMALE

aww...that cute little old lady is selling cartoon ghost books and stickers!

SHE'S LIKE A FUTURE ME ...IF I WAS FEMALE, JAPANESE, AND COULD DRAW BETTER!

(I bought the ghost with pancakes drawing of course)

...NOT TO MENTION ALL OF THE DIFFERENT GENRES OF COMICS AT COMIKET!

WOW! ANIMAL COMICS! SPORTS COMICS! CUTE COMICS! CREEPY COMICS! COMICS! COMICS! COMICS!

LEAVING THE CAT COMIC SECTION

ENTERING THE BIRD COMIC SECTION

MY JAPANESE ISN'T THE STRONGEST, BUT I SPEAK THE UNIVERSAL LANGUAGE OF ZILLA...

RAWR!!

RAWR!!

RAWR!

AGGGHH!! GOJIRA!!

← TABLES WERE ACTUALLY MUCH TINIER ...MAYBE 3 or 4 feet wide

ALTHOUGH I SADLY DIDN'T FIND ANYONE ELSE DRESSED LIKE GODZILLA, THERE WERE STILL PLENTY OF COSTUMES TO BE SEEN...

HA HA! YOU'RE A MARKER!! NICE COSTUME!!

YOU TOO!

MARKY'S SIDE

CHISEL TIP

MAR

I ALSO MANAGED TO GET YELLED AT FOR RUNNING UP THE ESCALATOR...

but ...I'm godzilla

...BUT SINCE MY JAPANESE VOCABULARY DOESN'T INCLUDE ADMONISHMENTS I HAD NO IDEA WHAT WAS SAID ...AND IF IT WAS EVEN DIRECTED AT ME...

THAT CHANGED THE SECOND TIME I GOT IN TROUBLE, AS THE OTHER PERSON KINDLY CLARIFIED FOR ME...

NO! WALK!

...but I'm godzilla

biggest escalator I've ever been on.

I REMAINED MOTIONLESS ON ALL ESCALATORS AFTER THAT

damian 2017 END

Watercolours.

This section collects a number of watercolours I had made while on the train in Japan (left), as well as a few of my favourite pieces from World Watercolour Month (some mixing horror movies with eggs - don't ask). The originators of World Watercolour Month at Doodlewash.com also kindly featured me as a guest artist on their site which is a great resource if you like watercolour.

"BIPOLAR BEAR"

"It's not that easy to Arcticulate"

The fateful meeting of penguins & polar bears.

"The Bird of Frankenstein"

"Dr. Frankenstein's Muenster"

"Fried Egg the 13th"

"The Hunchyolk of Notre Dame"

"Humpty Bogart"

"Alfregg Hitchcock"

"How my mind works"
This is actually quite accurate.

"Graceful Eggsit"

"Shell Shock"

"Whaling season wouldn't end well this year"

'CASH. MY WIFE SAID I'M CHARGING TOO MUCH'

"Paying though the nose"

This title might be a British expression ....it means paying too much.

"Silent Night"
(featuring Skully)

"The Twisty Part of my Bass Guitar"

"Lychee"

"Kiwi"

damian.

(notice the "Zilla" names on the cups)

Friggin' Hujezilla (left: official drinker of coffee & supplier of fun)
damianzilla (middle: official maker of ridiculous comics & bad puns)
Rachelzilla (right: official purveyor of cupcakes & zilla costumes)

damian willcox is an award nominated cartoonist that has been publishing his comics and artwork both in print and online for over twenty years.

During that time he has also written the Too Much Coffee Man Opera with Shannon Wheeler, survived his comics getting TV series related interest from Hollywood types, and has even appeared in a National Chinese television show as a 'wealthy foreigner'.

He currently lives in Calgary, Alberta, Canada and spends his days with his wonderful wife Miyuki and nutty dogs Lychee & Kiwi ("the fruits").

thanks for reading!

your comic friend,

♥damian

@dorkboycomics

facebook.com/dorkboycomic

instagram.com/dorkboycomics

damian@dorkboycomics.com

www.dorkboycomics.com

"I told you before, Francis... don't panda to your audience"

"The two stages of comic creation"

www.ingramcontent.com/pod-product-compliance
Lightning Source LLC
Chambersburg PA
CBHW061356090426
42739CB00003B/39